NICK BUTTERWORTH AND MICK INKPEN

THE LITTLE GATE

D1189076

To help people understand what God is like,
Jesus told lots of stories which are as exciting
today as when they were first heard.

The Little Gate is still a great favourite
and its message is one that children especially
love to hear.

This edition published by Candle Books in 2008,
a publishing imprint of Lion Hudson plc.

Distributed in the UK by Marston Book Services Ltd,
PO Box 269, Abingdon, Oxon OX14 4YN

Text and illustrations copyright © 1986, 1989 Nick Butterworth and Mick Inkpen.
First published by Marshall, Morgan & Scott.
Nick Butterworth and Mick Inkpen assert the moral right to be identified as the
authors and illustrators of this work.

Scripture quotations in this book are taken from the Good News Bible © 1966, 1971,
1976, 1992 American Bible Society.

All rights reserved. No part of this publication may be reproduced, stored in a
retrieval system, or transmitted in any form or by any means – electronic,
mechanical, photocopy, recording, or any other – except for brief quotations in
printed reviews, without the prior written permission of the publisher.

International publishing rights owned by Zondervan®.
Worldwide co-edition produced by Lion Hudson plc,
Wilkinson House, Jordan Hill Road, Oxford, OX2 8DR
Tel: +44 (0)1865 302750 Fax: +44 (0)1865 302757
Email: coed@lionhudson.com www.lionhudson.com

ISBN 978 1 85985 751 9

Printed in China

NICK BUTTERWORTH AND MICK INKPEN
THE LITTLE GATE

Here is a wall which surrounds a town.

In the wall is a little gate. It has a funny name. It is called the Eye of a Needle because it is so small.

One day a camel arrives at the gate.

This is no ordinary camel. He has a fine saddle with red tassles, and his own servant boy to flick away the flies.

He is loaded high with carpets to sell in the market.

'Make way,' he says, 'I'm coming through!'

But he isn't coming through at all! He can't get through the hole. He is too big!

'Try wriggling through
backwards,' says the boy.
And he shows the camel how.

'Camels never wriggle,' says the camel. But just the same, he turns around and pushes his bottom into the hole.

He heaves and pushes.
(He even wriggles.)

But it is no good. He cannot
get through the gate.

'I'll unload you,' says the boy. He unties the ropes and takes off all the carpets.

'Now try again.'

It is no use. The camel still cannot squeeze through the gate.

'Your saddle keeps getting stuck,' says the boy. 'You will have to let me take it off.'

Without his fine saddle, the camel does not look proud and important any more.

He is just an ordinary camel.

Once more the camel tries.
Down on his knees, shuffling
forward, inch by inch, until
finally . . .

Hooray! He is through!

Jesus says, 'It is very hard for a rich man to get into heaven. It's easier for a camel to get through the eye of a needle!'

Jesus said, 'It is much harder for a rich person to enter the Kingdom of God than for a camel to go through the eye of a needle.'

Mark 10:25

Other titles from **Candle Books** *by*
Nick Butterworth and Mick Inkpen

The House On The Rock
The Lost Sheep
The Precious Pearl
The Good Stranger
The Two Sons
The Rich Farmer
The Ten Silver Coins
The Little Gate

Stories Jesus Told
Animal Tales
Stories Jesus Told Colouring Book